THE PRINTED PATTERN

INTERIORS

THE PRINTED PATTERN

Techniques and Projects for Inspired Printmaking and Surface Design

Rebecca Drury and Yvonne Drury

Photography by Sophie Drury

First published in the United States in 2011 by

Interweave Press LLC
201 East Fourth Street
Loveland, CO 80537
Interweave.com

ISBN: 978-1-59668-386-0
CIP data not available at time of printing.

Printed and bound in China.

We would like to dedicate this book to all the people who have inspired and helped us over the years.

ACKNOWLEDGMENTS

This book would have never been possible if it was not for our photographer, Sophie, who spent countless hours trying to capture our vision.

A very special thank you to Lee and Chris for all their hard work, support, and advice.

Many thanks to Beejal who helped us with some of our projects.

MIXTURE
PIPE TOBACCO

INTRODUCTION

We love making patterns and designs. Developing new motifs and seeing them grow into designs is so exciting. You never know exactly how a design will turn out; you have an idea, which you develop into a pattern, and—voila!—a new design is born. You can then use this design to transform everyday items into very special objects.

Printed pattern can be applied to almost any surface, including fabric, paper, card, ceramics, glass, or wood. It can be easy and simple to achieve wonderful effects. Special equipment is not always necessary because you can print your own patterns inexpensively and effectively on a kitchen table or worktop at home. A vast array of patterns can be produced, from the textured effect of a linoprint to the crisp starkness of a screen print.

This book contains simple step-by-step instructions for various types of projects and methods—but mainly, it is filled with ideas and inspiration. By showing you how simple it can be to achieve impressive results, we hope to inspire you to explore the world of creating and printing your own patterns. Once you begin experimenting with different techniques, you will see that the possibilities are endless; experimentation is essential because it helps you to explore the processes. The projects that we have illustrated throughout this book are intended as starting points for your own designs. We hope this will help and encourage you to develop your own style.

We can guarantee that you will make mistakes along the way; even the most experienced designers and printers make mistakes. Try not to worry when you do. That is the nature of hand printing; things just do not always turn out the way you expect. Mistakes should not be treated as negative experiences because you can learn and develop your skills through them. Working out what went wrong, and why, helps you gain a deeper understanding of the techniques and processes. Sometimes, you will even enjoy nice surprises when your unintended outcomes result in "happy mistakes"—unexpected results that turn out to be fabulous.

You do not need any previous experience or knowledge to make a start on these projects.This book is suitable for anyone, from the absolute beginner to the more experienced. It is designed to help you develop and expand your skills and confidence. We believe that there is an element of creativity within everyone, and we hope that this book helps to release some of your potential. So give printed patterns a go!

INSPIRATION

Inspiration is all around us; colors, shapes, motifs, patterns and textures are all present both in nature, and in man-made environments. Recognizing these as potential sources of inspiration is simply about taking the time to pause and observe. Most of the time we are so busy getting on with things, rushing from one place to the next, that we just do not seem to notice what is around us. So stop for a second and take another look, whether it be in your garden, on your way to work, or while you are shopping. Interesting and unusual patterns, motifs, textures, and color combinations are to be found almost everywhere! You will be surprised at what you discover once you start looking and may find that you won't be able to stop.

A simple leaf or flower has so many beautiful qualities of line, shape, color, and texture. If your inspiration is taken from nature, your design is more than likely to have an organic feel. On the other hand, if you look toward man-made structures and the urban environment, your design may contain graphic lines and have a geometric structure. Sources of inspiration are everywhere. So unleash your creativity, take that second look. Rip up those paint charts and get creative using nature's own color palette and the objects and structures that surround you every day.

Designing your own motifs and patterns inspired by your environment means that the patterns you create will be individual to you; they will reflect who you are and enable you to put your personal stamp on items you are making and decorating. If you decide to use existing patterns and motifs, such as the ones included in the back of this book, you will still produce unique results because you will be using the motifs, choosing the colors, and printing and creating patterns by hand. Your arrangement and placement of the motifs and the colors and textures will have distinctive and special qualities. The outcome will be a unique handmade design.

Let the sunshine in!

TOILETTES
TELEPHONES
184 3/4
LAUNDRY
AND
DRY CLEANERS
302
RETOURNAG
ALEX
182429

359
TROPOLITA
LIQUORS

DEVELOPING IDEAS

Collating imagery

To begin creating your own designs, start collecting inspirational imagery. Keep records in the form of sketches, drawings, photographs, or found objects. To develop your collections of inspirational images into design ideas, create moodboards and sketchbooks.

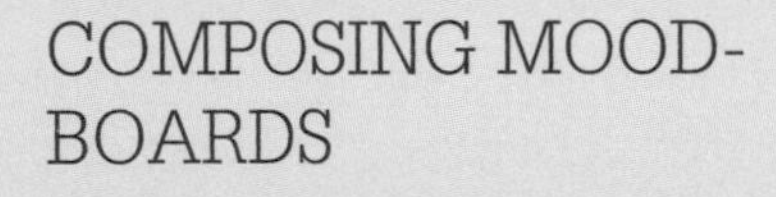

COMPOSING MOOD-BOARDS

A moodboard is a collage of images, text, colors, and textures. It is made up of visual information that captures the style and essence of your idea/concept. You can include a range of materials, such as printouts, magazine cutouts, photographs, textures, fabrics, and color palettes/chips. The collected items and materials are then carefully arranged and fixed in place on paper or card to create your moodboard.

BOLD
Les Trois

SKETCHBOOKS

You can use a sketchbook to collate your ideas, make notes, sketch, or paste in photographs and images from magazines. It is your own personal visual diary. Sketchbooks range in size. There are no rules; use whatever you feel most comfortable with.

COMPOSITION AND LAYOUT

When you start working on your designs, you need to think about the composition and layout you want to create. Your design should flow, without any awkward gaps or spaces, so you must consider the spacing between motifs and patterns. Try not to create layout ideas that are too complicated as often the simplest designs are the most effective. It is just a matter of striking the right balance between detail and simplicity. Once again, this is something that will improve with practice. Look at other designs that you like and try to analyze what it is that makes them successful in terms of composition and layout. There are many different types of layouts, such as stripes, borders, single motifs, and multiple allover patterns.

GETTING STARTED

It is essential to be well prepared before you begin. Expensive equipment is not required, but you will need some basic key tools and materials.

PRINTING SURFACE

A specially designed printing surface is not required; your kitchen or dining-room table or kitchen worktop will suffice. You can even print on the floor if you do not have a suitable tabletop. However, do bear in mind that if you are going to be printing for sustained periods of time, it is important you are in a comfortable position. You do not want be leaning over repeatedly or straining because you risk injuring your back!

What you need is a flat, even surface. If you are printing on paper or card, a hard surface is fine. However, if you are going to be printing on fabric, particularly using a silk screen, your printing surface should be slightly soft. It should have a little give. The easiest way to achieve this is to pad your surface; a blanket covered with either a cotton sheet or a piece of calico, then stretched over the tabletop, pulled taut, and secured works very well. Using a piece of plywood, chipboard, or medium-density fiberboard (MDF) and covering this with the blanket and calico is an even better idea. This you can pull tight, making sure it is wrinkle-free, and then fix it using a staple gun on the underside to secure the padding in place. This way, you will always have a printing surface ready. You can just place it on your table, worktop, or floor, and you are ready to go!

BASICS

You will need:

Water. Make sure you have a water supply close by. You will need water to clean your tools and equipment. Your kitchen sink, shower, and bath are all ideal water supplies.

Scrap paper/newspaper. Keep a plentiful supply of scrap paper; it is very useful to protect your work surface.

Cloths/rags. Paper/kitchen towel. These are great for cleaning up. You can never have too many cloths and rags!

Scissors or a sharp craft knife.

Old spoons and jars. These are useful for mixing and storing your inks and dyes. Start collecting!

Apron/old clothes and gloves. It is always a good idea to wear an apron or old clothes when you are printing. It can be a messy business!

Masking tape.

Hairdryer. A hairdryer is great for drying off your prints and equipment and speeding up the process.

MATERIALS

There is a vast array of materials available to print on: fabric, paper, card, wood, plastic, and ceramics are just a few. You can obtain all of these in a variety of surfaces, colors, and finishes; the choice is immense. When selecting materials or items do bear in mind that some are easier to print onto than others. Experience will teach you the pros and cons of printing on different materials and surfaces. However, it is good to keep an open mind and test and experiment with a variety of materials because sometimes the more challenging bases can provide the most interesting results.

Useful tips

- Always ensure you have extra materials so you can carry out test prints and experiment with samples before you start on your final pieces.

- White, natural, and lighter-colored materials are more straightforward to print onto. On these surfaces your print will really stand out. If you have a darker-colored material that you wish to work with, make sure that your ink/paint is opaque (rather than transparent); otherwise, your print may not show up.

- In general, it is easier to print onto flatter surfaces, i.e., those that are not too textured. That said, interesting results can be obtained on textured surfaces. Experimentation is the key here!

- When printing onto any products that have a back, such as bags, T-shirts, or cushions, you must always place a sheet of thin card inside, between the two layers. This will stop any ink seeping through onto the back layer.

INKS

As with the vast choice of possible materials, there is an extensive range of inks and dyes to choose from. You will find a suitable printing ink for each and every type of material you wish to print on.

Different inks have different characteristics, whether they are glossy, matte, opaque, or translucent. The main difference between inks is whether they are water-based or oil-based. We mainly use water-based inks to print on fabric; these are easier to clean off equipment and clothes. They are, in general, also more environmentally friendly.

Oil-based inks require special solvents for cleaning. Therefore, if using oil-based inks, make sure you work in a well-ventilated area. Oil-based inks are not suitable for processes such as potato printing because they do not stick to moist surfaces. You must also be careful to dispose of any waste in a responsible manner.

COLORS

Experiment with color. Finer colors can be achieved by mixing inks together, rather than just using the inks straight from the container. Instead of using a premixed green, for example, try mixing a green using yellow and blue. You can then add a little white to make the color paler and more pastel. Or add a little black if you want your color to be more muted.

Useful tips

- Always read the manufacturers' instructions and follow their directions closely.

- Try experimenting with small amounts first, to minimize waste.

- Strong or dark colors can have a dramatic effect when mixing inks; just a few drops can significantly change the look of the final color.

- When mixing, do not use too many colors because this always produces a muddy outcome.

- When mixing inks, use the same type of ink/dyes. For example, do not mix water-based ink with oil-based ink or gouache with acrylic.

- When mixing, keep a record of the colors and amounts you are using as you mix, so that you can replicate the final color if required.

- Always test your color on the material you are going to be using because the base color can significantly alter the color of the print.

RELIEF PRINTING

POTATO PRINTING

Potato printing is one of the easiest and most accessible methods of relief printing; it is also a simple and inexpensive technique. It represents a naïve, hand-printed style. However, that's not to say that it is just for children. If you choose the right pattern and consider your colors carefully, you can produce beautiful and tasteful results.

When selecting your motif to make the potato stamp, it is better to choose a design with simple shapes and lines because these are easy to cut. An elaborate pattern that is overly detailed does not work as well with potato printing because it is difficult to cut and can look messy.

CUSHION You can use a plain cushion or make your own cushion from scratch. You can be as adventurous as you like when selecting a design for a cushion. Repeating patterns and engineered prints both work well on cushions. Think about tying in colors from your home.

Materials list

Raw potatoes (baking potatoes work best)
Paints and inks
Paintbrushes and sponge
Linocutting/woodcutting tool
or small knife
Paper towel
Tracing paper
Pencil or pen
Fabric, paper (or whatever you are
printing on)

Preparing your potato

First, select your motif.

Cut the potato in half.

Dry out any moisture by placing the potato cut-side down on a paper towel.

Draw your motif onto the cut side of the potato with a pencil or marker. A soft dark pencil works best.

If you are not confident drawing the motif directly onto the potato, begin by drawing the motif onto tracing paper. Lay the tracing paper onto the cut side of the potato. Using a sharp pencil, punch a few holes outlining the motif, then remove the tracing paper. You should now be able to draw your design onto the potato by joining up the holes that you made.

Now take your knife or cutting tool and cut around your motif. Make sure your cut is deep enough (about ½" [1 cm] is fine).

Printing

Apply ink or paint to the potato stamp with a brush or sponge. Remember, the ink should be quite thick. If the ink is too thin, it will be very difficult to obtain a successful result.

Before you start, practice by testing your potato stamp on a scrap piece of similar material. This is also the time to experiment with different color combinations.

Once you are happy with your colors and the results of your test print, you can start to print your design. Remember, you need to apply more ink each time you print your motif.

Useful tips

- Try to use an even coating of ink; too much ink will make your print bleed around the edges. Not enough ink will result in a patchy print.
- Remember to apply gentle and even pressure. This can take a little time to perfect, but all it takes is practice.
- Reapply more ink each time you print your motif.
- If you notice that your potato stamp is beginning to lose definition, this could be caused by a buildup of ink. You will need to wipe and gently rinse your stamp, then dry it before continuing.
- Your stamp can be reused for different colors simply by cleaning and drying your potato.
- You can achieve interesting layout options by overprinting your motif. However, you must ensure that each layer is dry before you print on top.
- When printing products that have two layers or a back (bag, T-shirt, or cushion), you must place a sheet of thin card inside between the two layers. This will stop any ink seeping through onto the back layer of your product.
- Your potato stamp should last one or two days. To preserve it for longer, you can wrap it in cling film or seal it in a plastic bag and place it in your refrigerator (always clean the stamp before storing).
- Never use oil-based inks or paints when printing with potatoes because oil and water do not mix.

PEG BAGS These simple drawstring bags are useful for a range of things, from pegs to knick-knacks. They would make ideal gift bags.

PLACEMATS Printing your own placemats is a good way to brighten up mealtimes. The mats can be used as individual place-mats, scattered on the table, or used as centerpieces.

LINO PRINTING

Linoleum or lino was developed in the 1860s. Lino is made from a mixture of linseed oil, resin, and powdered cork with a hessian backing; it is usually gray or light brown in color. The linocut method of printmaking was first used in Germany in the early twentieth century.

Lino printing is a versatile and inexpensive method of printing pattern. It requires only a few tools but offers a wide range of results. Lino blocks can be used for printing onto either fabric or paper. Lino has a flat surface, so the marks you cut into it will have a crisp and distinctive character. It is suitable for broad, bold designs and motifs that do not contain fine lines. Unlike the potato, lino is quite durable so you will be able to re-use it many times.

Linocutting chisels or gouges are available in different sizes and have either a V- or U-shaped cutting edge. We suggest that you buy at least one of each shape, as this will enable you to achieve a broader range of marks. Ideally, buy a set that consists of both shapes and a selection of sizes. Lino and linocutting tools are readily available from most art and craft shops.

Make a gift even more special by adding a unique design.

Materials list

Lino
Linocutting tools
Paints and inks
Palette knife or spatula
Small roller
Tracing paper
Pencil or pen
Rolling pin

Making your print

Select your design or motif.

Draw your motif onto the lino block with a pencil or marker. A soft dark pencil works best.

If you would rather not draw the motif directly onto the lino, you can draw the motif onto tracing paper and then transfer the image onto the lino.

Take your cutting tool and cut around your motif. Cut away the negative area; this is the area you do not want to print. Make sure to always push the chisel or gouge away from yourself, rather than pulling it toward you, and try not to cut too deeply.

Once you are happy with your cut design, you are ready to apply the ink to the lino.

Mix your ink on a glass slab and spread it evenly to make a thin layer. Now take your roller and roll smoothly over the ink, then onto the lino several times in different directions to make sure you achieve an even coat.

Place the lino block face down on the paper or fabric. To print effectively, you must apply even pressure. You can do this with your roller or hand if your block is small. If your block is bigger, you can use a rolling pin. Make sure that the block does not move while you are printing with it; otherwise, your results will be blurred and smudged. Then carefully peel back the lino.

You will need to re-apply ink each time you print. You may get a buildup of ink in the cutaway areas, which can cause a loss of definition in your printed design. If this happens, wipe away any excess ink with a cloth or paper towel.

Once you have finished printing, wash your lino block and let it air dry thoroughly.

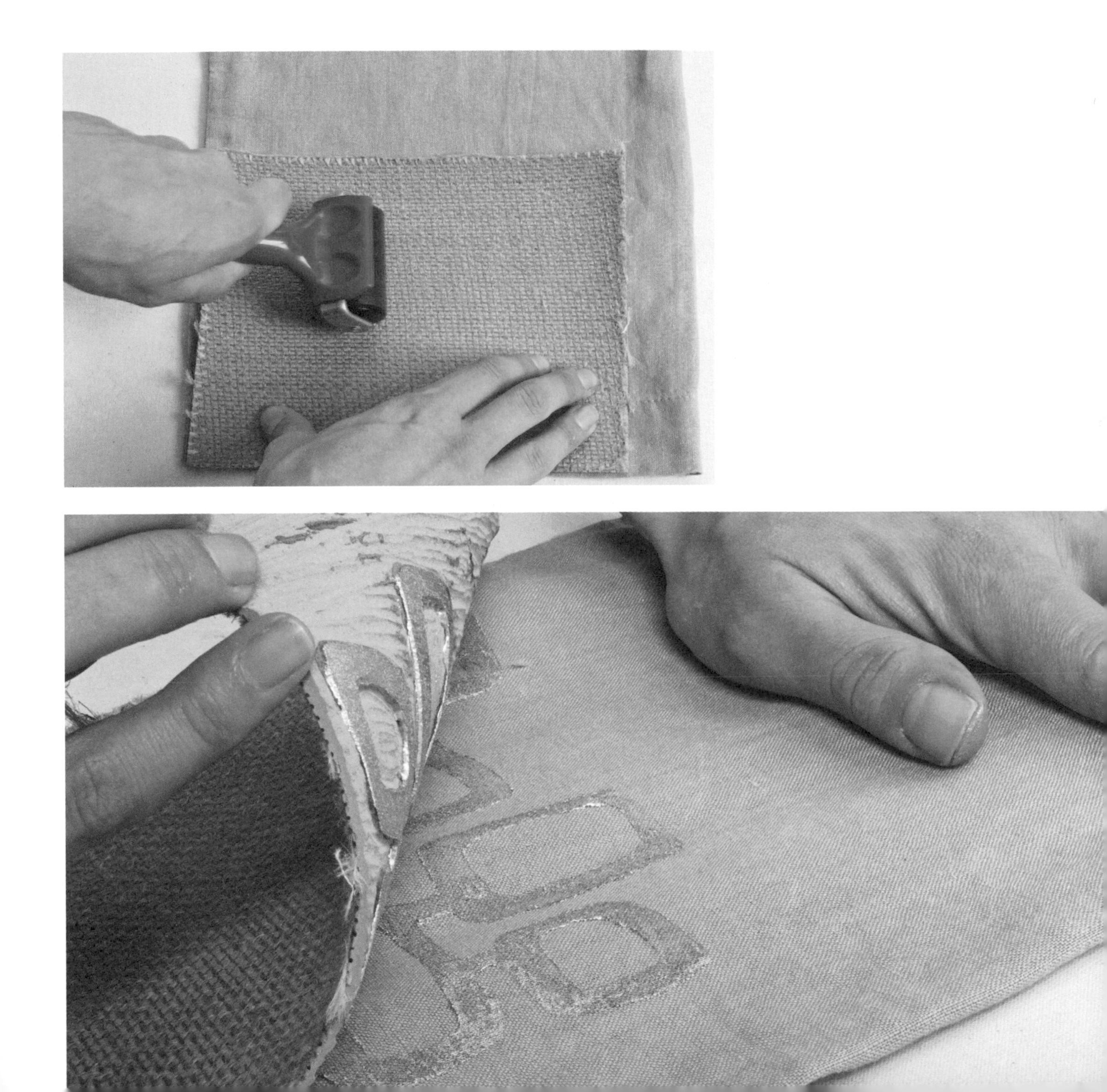

Useful tips

- Always test print first!

- Warm your lino by placing on a radiator or by using a hairdryer. This will make it easier to cut.

- To avoid injury, make sure that you always cut away from your body and keep your noncutting hand clear of the blade.

- To cut away large areas, use the U-shaped tool; to cut more precise details, use the V-shaped tool.

- Your linocutting tools will last a long time if you look after them. Do not store them with their blades rubbing against each other or any other metal objects because this will damage the cutting edge.

- A paper plate or an old kitchen chopping board can be used for rolling out your inks as an alternative to a piece of acrylic or glass.

Add some sparkle to a pair of trousers.

Personalize packaging or stationery using your own designs.

RUBBER/ERASER PRINTING

Rubber or plastic erasers can be used to make small, striking images. They are great fun. Once cut, they can be used to print on a variety of surfaces and may be re-used many times. If this method appeals to you, build up a collection that you can dip into to mix and match motifs. A motif created in this way can be used alone or repeated to make an allover pattern. Because erasers are quite small they are ideal for printing smaller items.

MURRAY'S
ERINMORE
MIXTURE
PIPE TOBACCO
NET WT 50 g
MIXTURE
VACUUM PACKED · TO OPEN · INSERT COIN AND TWIST

Materials list

Plastic or rubber eraser
Paints and inks
Paintbrushes/roller/ink block
Craft knife or lino-/wood-cutting tool
Paper towels
Tracing paper
Pencil
Fabric, paper (or whatever you are printing onto)

Making your print

Start by collecting a selection of plastic or rubber erasers. Try to select a few different shapes and sizes because doing so will provide a greater range of options for your designs and motifs. Long, thin erasers are good for stripe designs, while larger, square erasers lend themselves well to bigger motifs.

Select an eraser with at least one flat surface from which you can cut a motif.

Choose a motif and draw or trace it onto the flat side of the eraser with a pencil.

Use a craft knife or linocutting tools to cut around the edge of the design.

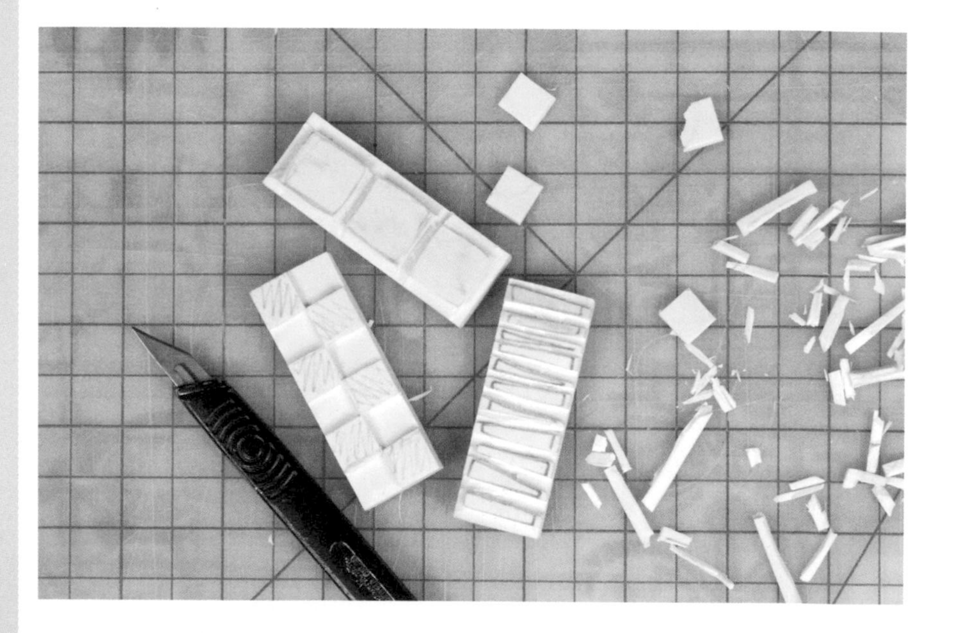

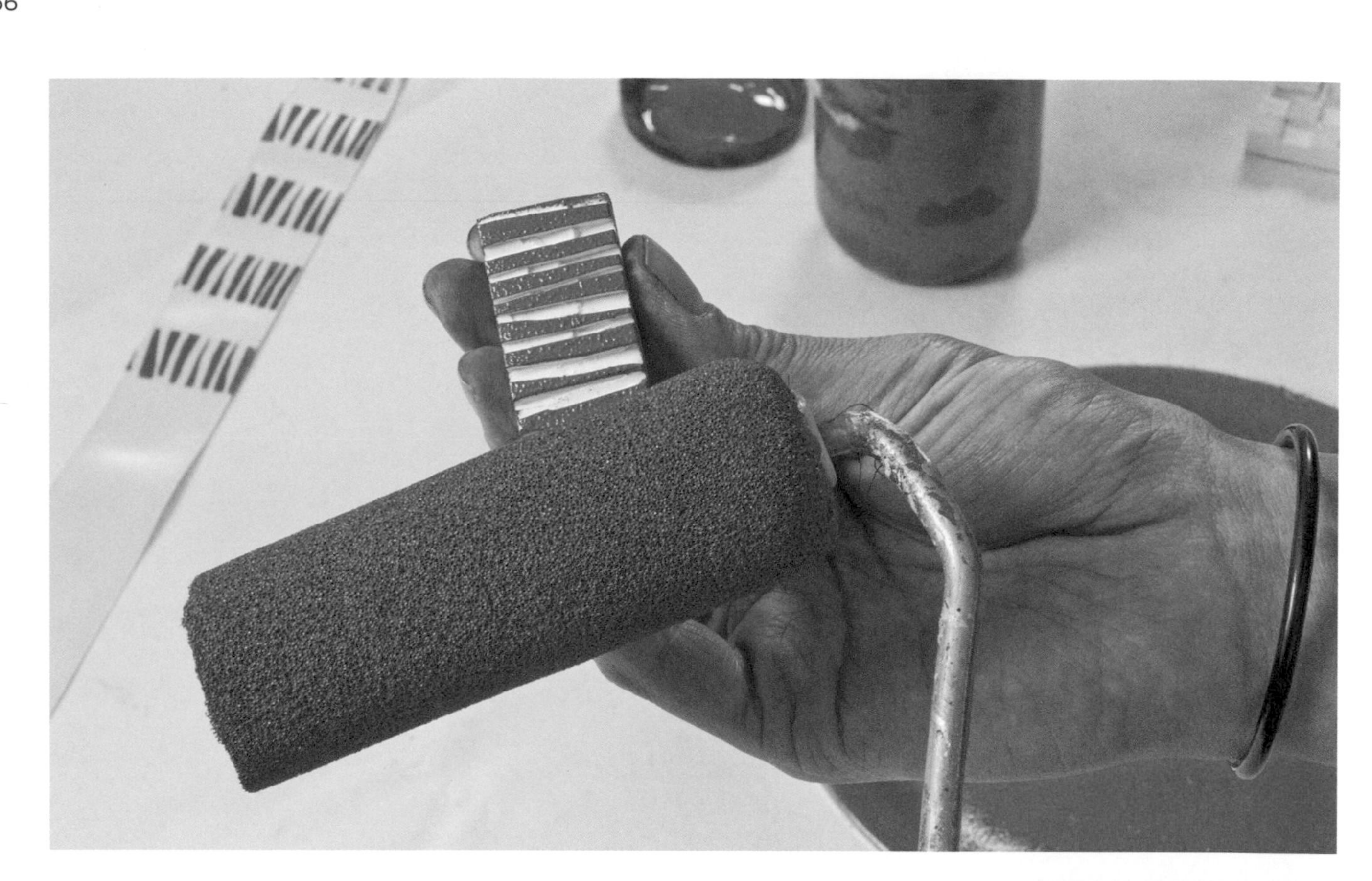

Apply your ink with a brush, roller, or inkpad.

To print, simply press the inked surface of the eraser down onto the material you wish to print on. Press firmly but not too hard. Remember to practice first on scrap paper or fabric.

Useful tips

- **Be careful when cutting out the design. Always cut away from your body to avoid accidents.**

- **Remember that the area that is cut away will be the negative area of your design, i.e., the part that won't print. The areas that remain once the cutting is complete form the motif that will print.**

- **Rubber erasers are a little easier to cut than plastic ones.**

Cheer up your kitchen cupboards with hand-printed paper labels.

Hand-printed ribbons add a finishing touch to that special gift.

Hand-printed gift tags are another way to personalize gifts for a special occasion.

RUBBER-STAMP PRINTING

This has to be one of the easiest and simplest printing methods of all. You can buy rubber stamps from art and craft and stationery shops. They are available in many designs and there is also a good choice of colored ink pads. Alternatively, you can easily have your own stamp made from your drawing or design.

You can make even a laundry bag special by being adventurous.

Materials list

Rubber stamp
Inkpad/sponge roller
Paper or fabric (or whatever you would like to print on)
Ink/paint

Rubber stamps can be printed onto a variety of surfaces. However, achieving a good result on very glossy or textured surfaces may prove more difficult.

Making your print

Ink your stamp by pressing it onto the inkpad or apply the ink directly to the stamp with a small sponge roller.

Press the stamp firmly onto the printing surface.

That's it!

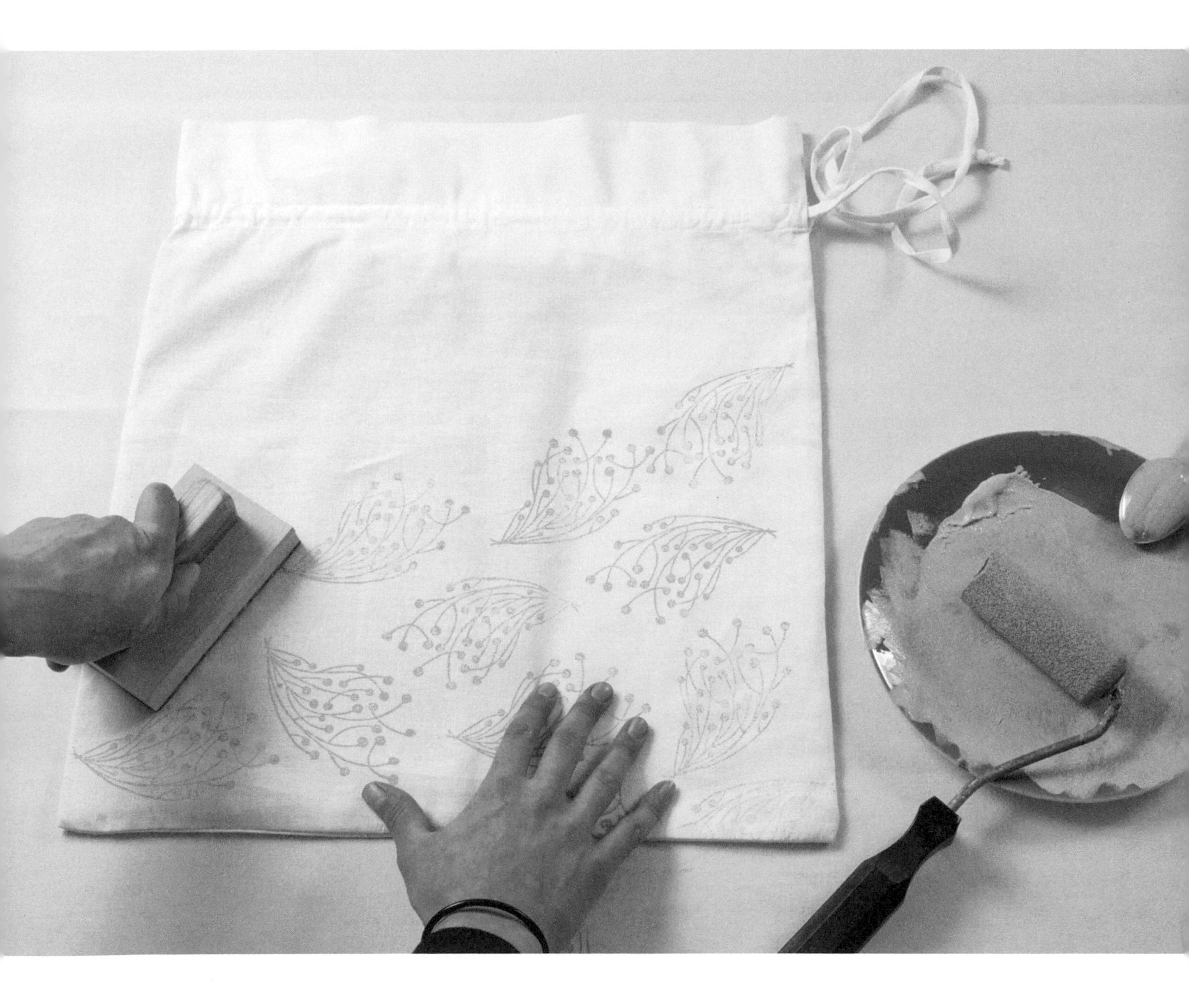

Useful tips

- Although this is a very simple method, you should still practice first. Different fabrics and materials require different pressure. By practicing first you will avoid unnecessary mistakes.

- After repeated printing, the stamp can get a buildup of ink on the backing and edges. If this happens, wipe the edges and backing with a clean cloth or kitchen towel before continuing.

- When you have finished printing with your stamp, wash it in warm water, blot it with a cloth, and allow it to completely air dry before re-using.

Make a unique statement by customizing a skirt.

Handmade cards show that you care.

VINTAGE WOODBLOCK PRINTING

Woodcutting is a much more complex and technical process than the others in this section, requiring specific tools and equipment. The actual engraving of the wooden block requires skill, time, and patience. Woodblock printing is an ancient process. Woodblocks are known to have existed in northern China since 627 AD. They were well established in Europe by the fifteenth century.

Vintage woodblocks can be found in antique shops, at flea markets, and on eBay. They can be brought to life again and re-used; by recycling in this ethical and interesting way, you can produce items that are not only unique but also very special.

Materials list

Vintage woodblock
Inks or inkpad/roller
Fabric, paper (or whatever you are printing onto)

Making your print

Ink up your woodblock by pressing it onto an inkpad or apply the ink directly to the woodblock using a small sponge roller. Be sure to do this evenly and smoothly.

Press the woodblock firmly onto your printing surface.

Useful tips

- **Refer to rubber-stamp printing; both methods have similar requirements.**

Make a gift extra special by wrapping it in your own woodblock-printed paper.

ROMAN BLINDS Vintage woodblocks can be used on most kinds of fabrics and papers. They are great for decorating plain objects such as these Roman blinds.

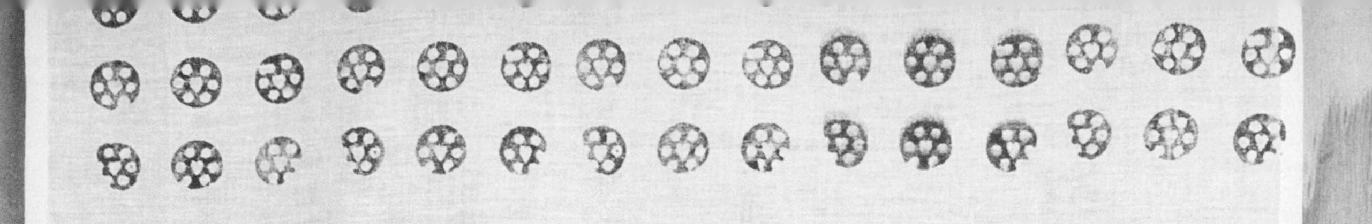

STENCIL PRINTING

Stenciling is a simple and basic print technique. However, it is exceptionally versatile and you can produce some stunning results. It is quite easy to make a stencil and once again it is a process that will not require too many specialized materials or equipment. Stenciling can be used on so many different surfaces—from paper and fabric to walls, floors, furniture, and accessories. The possibilities are endless.

Materials list

Thick paper or card, acetate, or Mylar
Permanent marker
Scalpel/craft knife
Cutting mat or a piece of thick card
Paints/inks
Masking tape
Stencil brush, sponge, or small sponge roller
Spray mount

You can cut your stencil from many different papers and plastics. The stencil will last longer if it is cut from a plastic-type material, such as acetate or Mylar. It will easily withstand repeated printing and you will be able to wash it and re-use it many times. Acetate is readily available from any stationery store. Mylar is a polyester film commonly used for stencil making and is sold at art supply stores. If you use acetate or Mylar, you will be able to spray the back of your stencil with spray mount. This will make it tacky so it adheres to the material you are printing on and will help stop leakages.

The material you are printing on determines the ink you will need for stencil printing. To apply the ink you can either use a stencil brush, a sponge, or a sponge roller. A stencil brush is cylindrical with a flat top, which you use to stipple the ink through the cut stencil. Stencil brushes are available in many different sizes so they can be used for small details or larger areas. A sponge can also be used to apply the ink; however, we prefer to use a small sponge-decorating roller. These can be purchased at any DIY or decorating store.

Preparing your stencil

Begin by drawing your design or motif in a sketchbook or on paper.

Once you have finalized your pattern or motif, photocopy your design (at this stage you have the opportunity to change the scale of it if you wish).

Lay the photocopy onto a cutting mat and stick it down at the corners to secure it. Place the acetate/Mylar on top, sticking this down in place as well to avoid any movement while you are cutting.

Now cut out the design using a sharp scalpel/craft knife; always use a cutting mat or a thick piece of card to protect the surface you are working on.

Printing

Position the cut stencil onto the material you will be printing on, then use either masking tape or spray mount to secure it.

Put the ink on a plate and load your brush, sponge, or roller with ink.

Apply the ink in thin coats to build up a layer. Applying too much ink all at once will result in an uneven print and could cause the design to bleed.

Carefully remove the stencil once the design/motif has been printed. If you plan to use more than one color or layer, always make sure the ink is dry before starting to print the next layer.

Useful tips

- Ink should not be too runny or thin because it will leak under the stencil and cause your design to bleed.

- Avoid designs with fine, delicate lines because they will prove too difficult to cut.

- Make sure that the sheet of card/acetate/Mylar is adequately larger than your chosen design/motif. It is important to have plenty of room around your motif to help protect the material you are printing on from splashes.

- If you use more than one color, it is best to have a different plate, brush, or sponge for each ink.

- Just before you use your acetate or Mylar stencil, spray it underneath with spray mount to make it slightly tacky. This will stop the ink from leaking underneath.

- If you are using spray mount, be careful because it is toxic. Avoid inhaling the fumes and wear a protective mask. Always use the spray outside.

- Spray mount may have to be reapplied once it has lost its tackiness.

LAMPSHADE A simple drum lampshade is ideal for stenciling because it has an even surface. Inspiration for this pattern came from the vintage base.

FABRIC WALL HANGING A wall hanging may be slightly more ambitious than you had planned for because of its scale. Don't let this put you off, just give it a go and you will be amazed with the results you can achieve.

CUSHION Why not experiment with different color layers. This two-color stencil creates a striking contrast on the white cushion.

SHOPPING BAG Do not discard your stencils; they can be re-used many times. Here we have re-used our stencil on a shopping bag; with a change of color, a whole new look is achieved.

SCREEN PRINTING

A variety of different techniques can be used when printing with a silk screen. Here we are going to cover the three main methods: stencil, screen filler, and photo emulsion. Screen printing is great fun and you can achieve some excellent results. The silk screen enables the ink to be distributed evenly and in a controlled manner.

STENCIL-METHOD SCREEN PRINTING

This is a good method for a beginner. It is the simplest and least expensive way to prepare a screen. By cutting a stencil from paper or acetate, you can achieve bold and dynamic results. Designs can be cut with scissors, a knife, or alternatively, they can be torn to create a textured look. This technique works best with designs and motifs that are bold and do not have too much detail.

Once you have prepared your screen, you can work quickly to produce repeat prints one after the other. You can also achieve a high level of detail, especially when using the photo-emulsion method.

Screen printing is easy to do at home. Screens, inks, and equipment can be purchased from any good art and craft supplier. You can print on your kitchen or dining room table and wash off your screen in the kitchen sink or bath.

WALLPAPER/WALL HANGING Hand-printed wallpaper can transform any room. By screen-printing a design onto a roll of plain wallpaper, you can bring color and pattern into your surroundings.

STENCIL METHOD

Materials list

Newspaper/newsprint or acetate
Scissors or craft knife
Silk screen
Squeegee
Inks or paints
Masking tape
Pencil or pen
Fabric, paper (or whatever you are printing on)

Preparing your screen

First of all, select your design; remember to choose something without fine detail.

Draw your design onto the newspaper/newsprint or acetate. You can create a freehand design or trace an image using tracing paper.

Now cut out your design or tear the paper (tearing will create a textured edge to your design).

You can only use your newspaper/newsprint stencil a few times, so you will have to cut more than one. Acetate will last a lot longer; it can be washed and re-used many times.

Attach the stencil to the back of the screen with masking tape.

You are now ready to start test printing. See printing directions on p. 104.

Useful tips

- If using paper, keep it flat and make sure it is not wrinkled.

- Newspaper or newsprint works well for making stencils, but acetate gives better accuracy and durability.

- Your stencils should be slightly smaller than your screen frame.

- Remember to block out any areas in your screen that are not covered by the stencil; otherwise, the ink will get through and could ruin your print.

- You may be able to use a paper stencil again if it has not moved and is still intact.

TEA TOWEL Add a little character to those plain kitchen tea towels. These would also make ideal gifts!

SCREEN-FILLER METHOD

Using the screen-filler method is another simple way of preparing a screen for printing. The screen filler is painted directly onto the screen to block out those areas you do not wish to print. The ink is forced through the screen in areas where the screen filler has not been applied. This method allows you to use the same design again and again.

ROLLER BLIND Bring the outside in by printing a nature-inspired print on a roller blind.

SCREEN-FILLER METHOD

Materials list

Soft pencil
Silk screen
Screen filler
Brushes

Preparing your screen

Take a sheet of plain paper and draw your design.

Place this layout on a table, then put your screen over this layout and trace your design directly on the screen mesh with a soft lead pencil.

Select an appropriate brush, because the brush will determine the type of line or texture produced. With a finer brush you will be able to achieve a more detailed design.

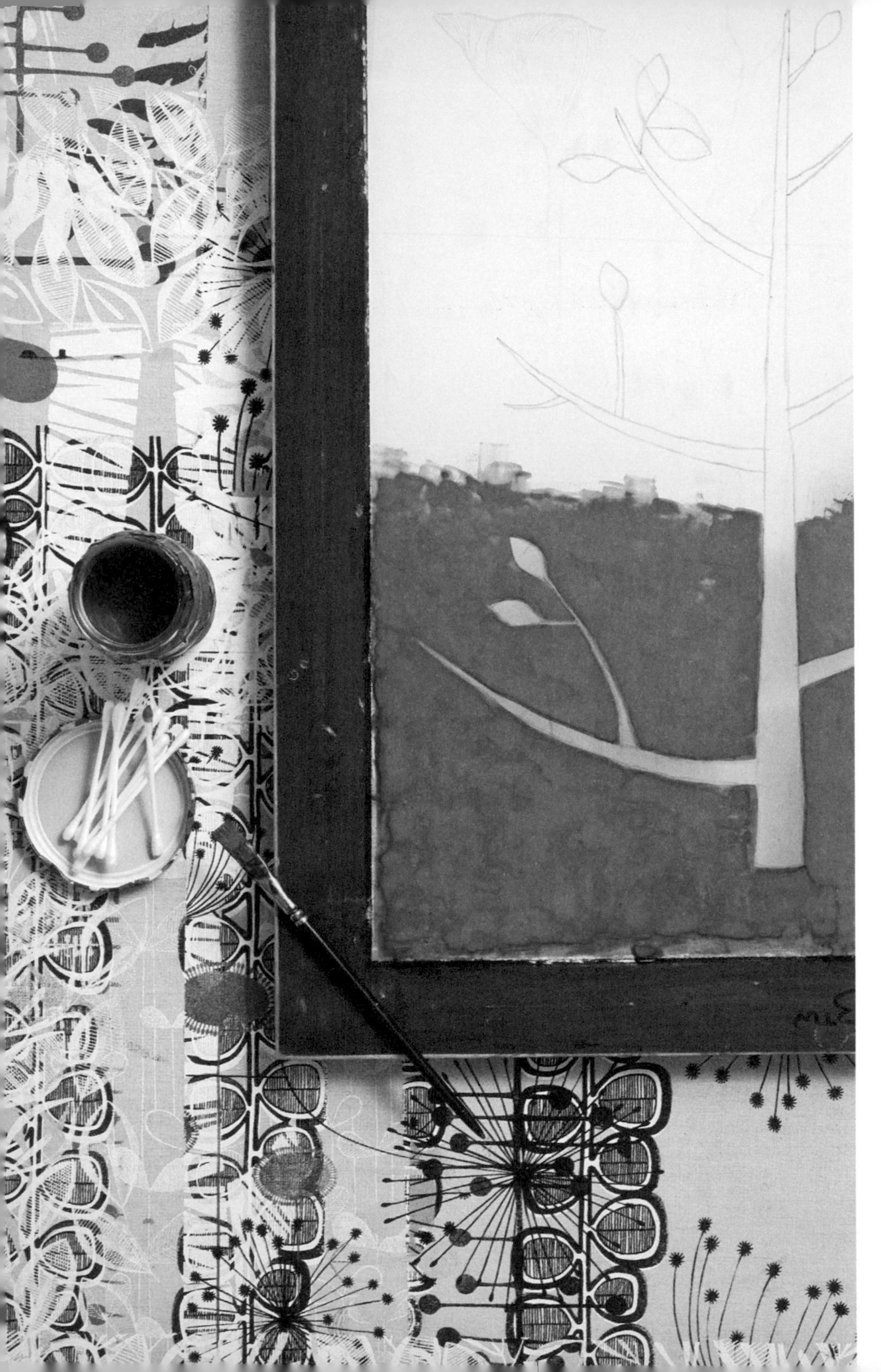

Working on the back of the screen, paint the areas of the layout that you do not wish to print. Turn the screen around and brush in any excess screen filler that has seeped through, making sure that it is even on both sides. When all areas to be blocked out are covered with screen filler, let the screen dry.

Now hold the screen up to the light to make sure you haven't missed any areas you wanted to cover. If you find any pinholes, you will need to spot these in with filler.

Leave to dry thoroughly, preferably overnight.

Your screen is now ready to use; see the printing directions on p. 104.

Useful tips

- **Always read the instructions on the screen filler or emulsion and activator bottles and follow them carefully.**

PHOTO-EMULSION METHOD

Using this technique, you can achieve a high level of detail. Your designs can include fine lines, photographic detail, and text. This method may require more preparation and equipment, but the outcome possibilities are far greater.

PHOTO-EMULSION METHOD

Materials list

Silk screen
Photo-emulsion kit
Squeegee or piece of card
Artwork (an image of your pattern or motif, printed in black on a clear acetate)
A clear flat piece of glass or Plexiglass (no larger than your screen)
Black paper (larger than your screen)
Light source (a clear, incandescent 150-watt bulb)

Preparing your screen

Place your screen on a flat surface with the top facing up (mesh side up).

Pour a little the emulsion onto the screen and, using a squeegee or a piece of card, spread it as evenly as possible. Don't put it on too thickly. You need as thin and even a coat as possible. Any excess can be scooped back into the pot of emulsion. You don't have to be a perfectionist. Just do your best.

Once the screen is coated, put it in a dark place to dry.

As soon as your screen is dry, you are ready to move on to the next step and expose your image. Do not leave your screen for too long or the emulsion will bake on and you will have to start over again.

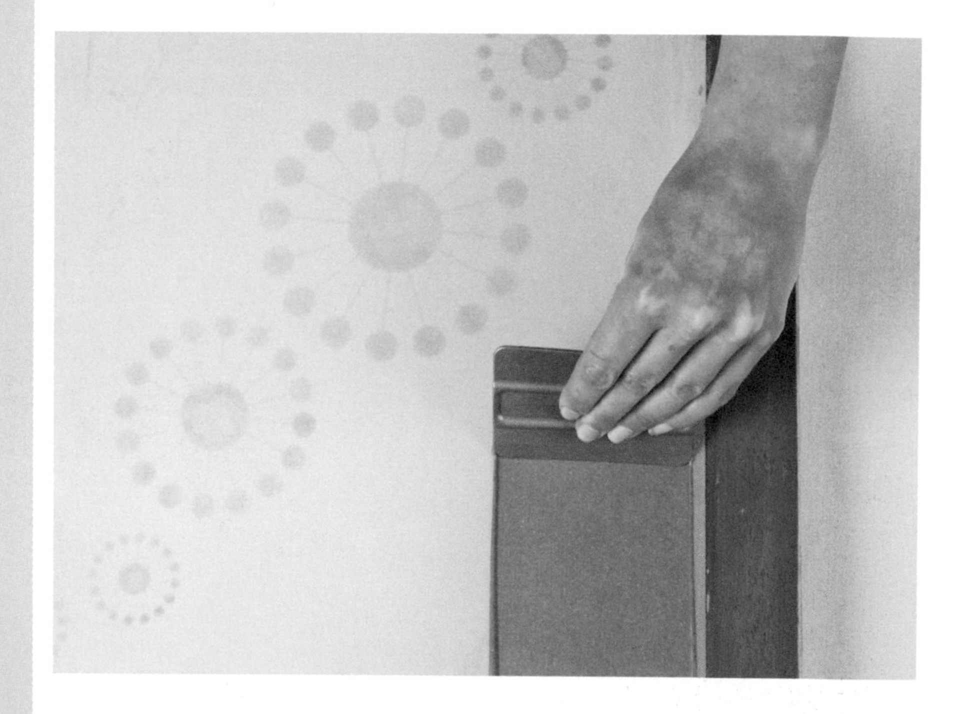

Exposing your screen

Make sure you are prepared with all your materials nearby; once you get the screen out of the dark, you need to work swiftly because it will be very sensitive to the light.

Place the screen flat on the piece of black paper with the coated side facing up. The light should be centered above the screen. Do not switch on the light just yet.

Place your artwork on the screen and lay the sheet of glass/Plexiglass directly over the top. Make sure you lay the artwork the correct way. This is especially important if you are using text in your imagery; the text could read backward if not positioned correctly.

You are now ready to expose your screen. Turn on the light, making sure the light bathes the whole screen.

The exposure time depends on the size of the screen. The following chart offers guidance for timings.

SCREEN SIZE	TIME
8" x 10" (20.5 x 25.5 cm)	45 minutes
10" x 14" (25.5 x 35.5 cm)	45 minutes
12" x 18" (30.5 x 45.5 cm)	74 minutes
16" x 20" (40.5 x 51 cm)	92 minutes
18" x 20" (45.5 x 51 cm)	92 minutes

Once you have exposed your screen, you need to wash it off.

Using a hose, spray your screen with cold water. You will be washing away the emulsion that has been protected by your artwork and so not been hardened by exposure to the light. You can also rub the screen gently to remove any excess emulsion.

You should now see your design being revealed. The design should be the same on your screen as on your artwork.

Now dry your screen; you can use a hairdryer to speed up the process.

When your screen is dry, hold it up to the light and check for any areas or pinholes the emulsion has missed. You can fill these using a small brush and some emulsion.

You are now ready to print.

Useful tips

- Follow the instructions on your photo-emulsion kit. Details will differ between alternative brands and types.

- When you dry your screen, a fan heater helps speed up the process.

- Always make sure that your screen artwork is as black as possible because you do not want the light to penetrate through it. If any light penetrates your design, your screen will be ruined and you will have to start again.

- Exposure times can vary depending on elements such as bulb wattage and the distance of the bulb from the screen. Be prepared to experiment with exposure timings.

- If you do not expose a screen for sufficient time, the image will wash away. If you expose a screen for too long, you will start to lose the fine detail of the image.

- You can expose your screen outside in the sun. Even on a cloudy day, there are plenty of UV rays you can use to achieve screen exposure.

- If there are areas your emulsion did not wash away from or in which too much emulsion washed away, you will have to clean your screen and start over again.

PRINTING WITH A SCREEN

Now here is the fun part—printing with your screen. Whichever screen printing methods you are using, the basics for printing with a screen are the same.

NECKTIES Even the dullest items can be brought to life and jazzed up using screen printing.

Materials list

Silk screen
Fabric or paper
Masking tape
Squeegee
Inks or paints
Spoon
Rags
Newspaper
Weights to hold down the screen

You will need to prepare an area to print on. Any tabletop is fine. When you print on fabric, your printing surface needs to be slightly soft; it needs to have a little give. So your tabletop/printing area will need padding. A good way to achieve this is to use a blanket with a sheet or a piece of fabric over the top. This should be pulled tight and secured under the table to give a taut, even surface.

As with any new method, screen printing takes practice; do not worry about making mistakes.

Before you start, practice by testing on a scrap piece of similar material. This is also the time to experiment with different color combinations and layering.

Once you are happy with your colors and the results of your test print, you can start to print your design.

Lay fabric or paper on the prepared tabletop and secure it with masking tape. This stops any movement while printing. Movement can cause blurred results.

Place and position your screen onto the fabric.

Put some weights on the corners of your screen to stop movement when printing. We use bricks wrapped in old tea towels or old weights.

Now place your squeegee at the top end of the screen and spread the ink along below the blade of the squeegee. Holding the squeegee firmly at a 45-degree angle, pull the ink firmly, quickly, and smoothly across the screen. You may need more than one pull so be prepared to repeat this two or three times depending on the ink and the type of fabric you are using.

Carefully lift the screen away from the fabric. Now that you can see the results of your print, you can evaluate whether you need to adjust your printing method. If your print has bled, you may have pressed too hard or used too many pulls. If your print is thin or patchy, this may be because of uneven pressure or not enough pulls.

Once you have finished printing, wash your screen and squeegee as soon as possible to avoid blocking the screen.

Useful tips

- Use gum strip to tape around the edges of your screen (this will stop the ink seeping through any cracks or gaps between the mesh and the frame). This is the best tape to use because other sticky tapes can leave a glue residue that is difficult to remove and can damage your screen.

- Experiment. Combine and overprint different motifs together.

- If you are using more than one color in your design, you will have to use a separate screen or different areas of a large screen for each different color/layer.

- Make sure that the ink on your first print is dry before you apply another color/layer.

- Always start printing with the lightest color and build up to darker colors, so that any overprinting is successful.

APRON Spice up mealtime with a hand-printed apron.

TABLE RUNNER & NAPKINS Why not revamp a plain table runner and napkins. It will add that something special to a dinner party.

VINTAGE CHAIRS Why not give vintage chairs a new lease on life by recovering them in handprinted fabric. Remove the old material to use as a template. Cut and print your fabric, then simply staple or tack your new fabric into place.

VINTAGE SOFA Once you have mastered screen printing, you may feel ready to take on something on a grander scale. Here we simply printed a large piece of fabric and then gave everything to a professional upholsterer. The upholsterer can advise on how much fabric is required.

STENCILS

The following pages contain seven stencils that are ready to use for your own printing and pattern-making. You can cut them out or copy them as you wish—and use them to inspire your own designs.

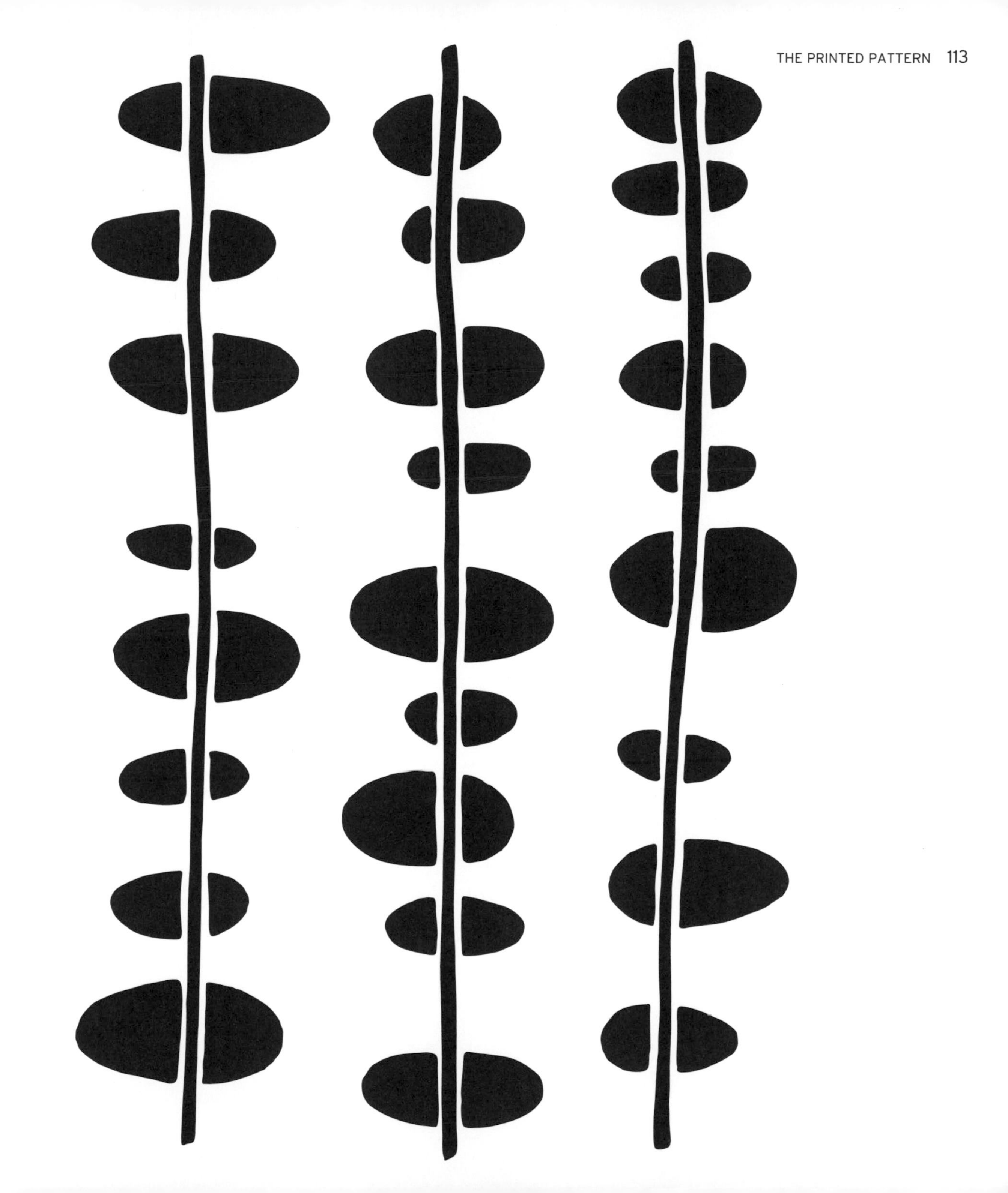

SUPPLIERS

USA

Atlantic Papers
1800 Mearns Rd., Ste. P
Ivyland, PA 18974
atlanticpapers.com
(800) 367-8547
Fine art papers

Blue Prints on Fabric
20504 81st Ave.
Vashon Island, WA 98070
(800) 631-3369
blueprintsonfabric.com
Sun-printing solutions, pretreated paper and fabric

Daniel Smith Inc.
PO Box 84268
Seattle, WA 98124
(800) 426-7923
danielsmith.com
Relief and monoprint inks, blocks, and carving tools

Dharma Trading Co.
PO Box 150916
San Rafael, CA 94915
(800) 542-5227
dharmatrading.com
Screen-printing ink, tools for printing on fabric, instructional material, pretreated paper and fabric

Dick Blick Art Materials
PO Box 1267
Galesburg, IL 61402
(800) 828-4548
dickblick.com
Block- and screen-printing inks, carving tools, relief blocks, frames, photo-emulsion solution, and exposure units

EZ Screenprint LLC
PO Box 10414
Casa Grande, AZ 85130
ezscreenprint.com
(520) 423-0409
Screen printing supplies

Graphic Chemical & Ink Co.
732 North Yale Ave.
Villa Park, IL 60181
(630) 832-6004
graphicchemical.com
Inks and tools for relief printing, screen printing, and monoprinting

KIWO Inc.
1929 Marvin Cir.
Seabrook, TX 77586
(800) KIWO-USA
kiwo.com
Photo emulsion, photo-emulsion cleaning solution

Nasco
901 Janesville Ave.
Fort Atkinson, WI 53538
(800) 558-9595
enasco.com/artsandcrafts
Block- and monoprint-printing inks, carving tools, blocks, pretreated paper for sun printing

Pearlpaint
pearlpaint.com
(800) 451-7327
Fine art and craft supplies

Speedball
2301 Speedball Rd.
Statesville, NC 28677
(800) 898-7224
speedballart.com
Block- and screen-printing inks, blocks, drawing fluid, screen filler, frames, squeegees, photo-emulsion solution, speed cleaner, instructional materials, kits.

Welsh Products Inc. (WPI)
1316 Oak Cir.
Arnold, CA 95223
welshproducts.com
Thermograph machines, mesh, frames, inks, instructional media.

UK

Atlantis Art Materials
7-9 Plumber's Row
London E1 1EQ
atlantisart.co.uk
020 7377 8855
Arts, painting and craft supplies

Colourcraft (C&A) Ltd
Unit 5,
555 Carlisle St. E.,
Sheffield S4 8DT
colourcraftltd.com
0114 242 1431
Dyes, printing inks, batiks, specialty inks

Cornelissen and Son Ltd
105 Great Russell St.
London WC1B 3RY
cornellisen.com
020 7636 1045
Printmaking supplies

Fibrecrafts and George Weil
Old Portsmouth Rd.
Peamarsh
Guildford
Surrey GU3 1LZ
georgeweil.co.uk
01483 565 800
Dyes, inks, fabrics, and equipment

Fred Aldous Ltd
37 Lever St.
Manchester M1 1LW
fredaldous.co.uk
0161 236 4224
Art, craft, and design supplies

London Graphic Centre
16-18 Shelton St.
Covent Garden
London WC2H 9JL
londongraphics.co.uk
020 7759 4500
Art, paper, and screen-printing supplies

Paintworks Ltd
99-101 Kingsland Road
London E2 8AG
paintworks.biz
020 7729 7451
Art and printmaking supplies, paper

Pongees
28-30 Hoxton Sq.
London N1 6NN
pongees.co.uk
020 7739 9130
Silk fabrics

R. K. Burt & Company Ltd
57 Union St.
London SE1 1SG
rkburt.com
020 7407 6474
Art papers

Selectasine Sergraphics Ltd
65 Chislehurst Rd.
Chislehurst
Kent BR7 5NP
selectasine.com
020 8467 8544
Silkscreens, squeegees, emulsion, printing inks

Thomas and Vines Ltd
Unit 5 & 6
Sutherland Court
Moor Park Industrial Centre
Tolpits Lane
Watford WD18 9SP
flocking.co.uk
01923 775111
Adhesives for fabrics

Tonertex Foils Ltd
PO Box 3746
London N2 9DE
tonertex.com
0208 444 1992
Foil papers and glitters

Explore the irresistible possibilities of surface design and mixed media

with these other inspirational resources from Interweave

Art Cloth
A Guide to Surface Design for Fabric
Jane Dunnewold

ISBN 978-1-59668-195-8
$26.95

Printmaking + Mixed Media
Simple Techniques for Paper and Fabric
Dorit Elisha

ISBN 978-1-59668-095-1
$22.95

The Surface Designer's Handbook
Dyeing, Printing, Painting, and Creating Resists on Fabric
Holly Brackmann

ISBN 978-1-931499-90-3
$29.95

The magazine for both beginner and seasoned artists interested in trying new techniques and sharing their work and expertise with a greater audience. Subscribe at **clothpaperscissors.com**

ClothPaperScissors.com is the online community where mixed-media artists come to play and share creative ideas. Receive expert tips and techniques, e-newsletters, blogs, forums, videos, special offers, and more! Join today.